KINGFISHER
LONDON & NEW YORK

This selection copyright © Kingfisher 2011
Illustrations copyright © Martin Chatterton 2006
Published in the United States by Kingfisher,
175 Fifth Ave., New York, NY 10010
Kingfisher is an imprint of Macmillan Children's Books, London.
All rights reserved.

First published 2006
This edition published 2011

Distributed in the U.S. by Macmillan,
175 Fifth Ave., New York, NY 10010

Library of Congress Cataloging-in-Publication data
has been applied for.

ISBN: 978-0-7534-6594-3

Kingfisher books are available for special promotions and
premiums. For details contact: Special Markets Department,
Macmillan, 175 Fifth Ave., New York, NY 10010.

For more information, please visit www.kingfisherbooks.com

Printed in the U.K. by CPI Mackays, Chatham ME5 8TD
2 4 6 8 10 9 7 5 3 1
0411

OVER
150
SPOOKY
JOKES!

Illustrated by **Martin Chatterton**

KINGFISHER
NEW YORK

**What is a baby ghost's
favorite game?**
Peeka-boo.

**What's the difference
between a deer
running away
and a small witch?**
*One's a hunted stag; the
other's a stunted hag.*

**What is a vampire's
favorite type of
ice cream?**
Veinilla.

**Why do witches fly
on broomsticks?**
*Vacuum cleaners' cords
aren't long enough.*

**What do zombies
like to eat at
barbecues?**
Halloweenies.

**Why didn't the skeleton
cross the road?**
He didn't have the guts.

What type of dog do vampires like best?
Bloodhounds.

Do zombies eat popcorn with their fingers?
No, they eat the fingers separately.

What kind of ghosts haunt skyscrapers?
High spirits.

**What's a monster's
favorite bean?**
A human bean.

**What happened when
the little witch
misbehaved at school?**
She was ex-spelled.

**What's red, sweet,
and bites people?**
A jampire.

Why do mummies have trouble keeping friends?
They're too wrapped up in themselves.

How do ghosts like their eggs?
Terri-fried!

What do you call a dead chicken that likes to scare people?
A poultry-geist.

Mommy, Mommy, all the kids call me a werewolf!
Never mind, dear. Now go and comb your face.

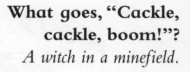

What goes, "Cackle, cackle, boom!"?
A witch in a minefield.

Why wasn't the vampire working?
He was on a coffin break.

What do skeletons say before eating?
"Bone appetit!"

What did one ghost say to the other ghost?
"Do you believe in people?"

**What type of
streets do zombies
like best?**
Dead ends.

**Why did the vampire
go to the orthodontist?**
To improve his bite.

**How do witches
keep their hair in
place while flying?**
With scare spray.

11

What did the daddy ghost say to his family when they were in the car?
"Fasten your sheet belts."

Why don't skeletons ever go out on the town?
Because they don't have any body to go out with.

What is evil, ugly, and goes around and around?
A witch in a revolving door.

What happens when a ghost gets lost in the fog?
He is mist.

How did the glamorous ghoul make a living?
She was a cover ghoul!

What do you get if you cross a vampire and a snowman?
Frostbite.

**What do they teach
at witch school?**
Spell-ing.

**What did Dracula
say when his
vampire girlfriend
kissed him?**
"Ouch."

**What did the
skeleton say to
the bartender?**
*"I'll have two Cokes
and a mop."*

**What's big and green
and goes, "Oink, oink?"**
Frankenswine.

**What's a vampire's
favorite dance?**
The fang-dango.

**What do ghosts
eat for dessert?**
Ice scream.

Why did the witch wash her broom?
She wanted a clean sweep.

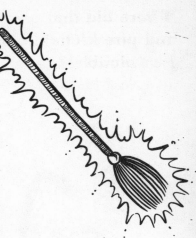

Who was the famous skeleton detective?
Sherlock Bones.

What do you call a lost monster?
A where-wolf.

Where did the vampire keep his valuables?
In a blood bank.

Why don't mummies go on vacation?
They're afraid they'll relax and unwind.

What does a ghost get when he falls and scrapes his knee?
A boo-boo.

**What do witches
have races on?**
Brrrroomsticks!

**What happened to
the wolf that fell into
a washing machine?**
*He became a
wash-and-werewolf.*

**What is a skeleton's
favorite musical
instrument?**
A trombone.

How does a female vampire flirt?
She bats her eyes.

Why didn't the witch wear a cap?
Because there was no point.

**What does a
skeleton order
in a restaurant?**
Spareribs.

**What do young
ghouls do their
homework in?**
Exorcise books!

**How can you tell if
witches are carrying
time bombs?**
*You can hear their
brooms tick.*

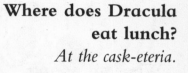

**Where does Dracula
eat lunch?**
At the cask-eteria.

What kind of ghost has the best hearing?
The eeriest!

Who won the skeletons' beauty contest?
No body.

What did the mummy say to the detective?
"Let's wrap up this case."

How did the witches' basketball team do?
They had a spell in the first division.

What is a mummy's favorite type of music?
Wrap!

Why doesn't anybody like Dracula?
He has a bat temper.

What ride do spirits like best at the amusement park?
The roller ghoster.

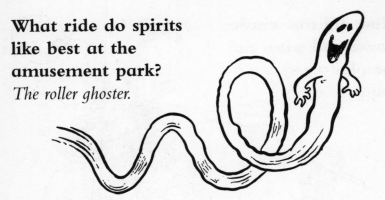

Why did the one-eyed monster have to close his school?
He only had one pupil.

How do you join the Dracula fan club?
Send in your name, address, and blood type.

What type of music do witches play on the piano?
Hagtime.

What were the results of the vampires' marathon?
It finished neck and neck.

What type of pets do ghosts have?
Scaredy-cats.

How do you make a witch scratch?
Just take away the "w."

Why do skeletons hate the winter?
Because the cold goes right through them!

Why shouldn't you grab a werewolf by its tail?

It might be the werewolf's tail, but it could be the end of you!

Why did the ghost starch her sheet?

So she could scare everyone stiff.

**Have you heard about
the good weather witch?**
She's forecasting sunny spells.

**Where does a ghost go
on Saturday nights?**
*Anywhere that he
can boo-gie.*

**Why does Dracula
go to art classes?**
He likes to draw blood.

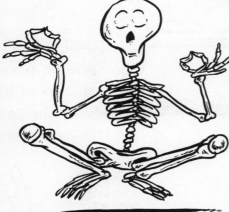

**Why are skeletons
so calm?**
*Nothing gets under
their skin.*

**What was the cold,
evil candle called?**
*The Wicked Wick
of the North.*

Why don't angry witches ride their brooms?
They're afraid of flying off the handle.

What does a ghost have on top of his ice-cream sundae?
Whipped scream.

What do you get if you cross Dracula with Sir Lancelot?
A bite in shining armor.

What do you call a monster with no neck?
The Lost Neck Monster.

Why are so few ghosts arrested?
It's impossible to pin anything on them.

Why did the skeleton jump on a trampoline?
To have a rattling good time!

Why did the vampires cancel their baseball game?
They couldn't find their bats.

How do you get milk from a witch's cat?
Steal her saucer!

Ghost: Where do fleas go in the winter?
Werewolf: Search me!

What has six legs and flies?
A witch giving her cat a ride on her broomstick.

What did the baby vampire bat say before going to bed?
"Turn on the dark. I'm afraid of the light!"

What do you call a stupid skeleton?
Bonehead.

What does a child monster call his parents?
Mommy and Deady.

What type of ghosts haunt operating rooms?

Surgical spirits!

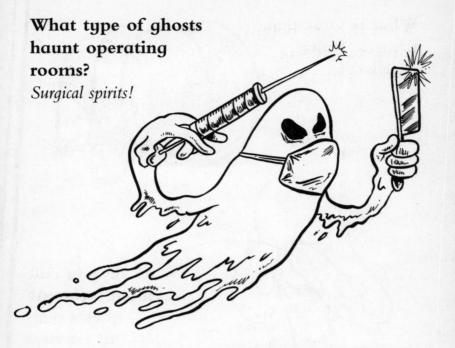

Why did the witch celebrate?

She passed her hex-ams.

What is Dracula's favorite fruit?
A neck-tarine.

What game do ghosts play at parties?
Hide-and-shriek.

What is as sharp as a vampire's fang?
His other fang.

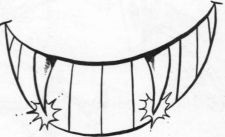

What type of jewelry do witches wear?
Charm bracelets.

What do you do when 50 zombies surround your house?
Hope that it's Halloween!

Where do ghosts go to mail their letters?
The ghost office.

What do you call a witch who lives at the beach?
A sand-witch.

Why are vampires like false teeth?
They only come out at night.

Why do demons and ghouls hang out together?
Because demons are a ghoul's best friend!

Why did the game warden arrest the ghost?
He didn't have a haunting license.

**What do you get if
you cross a witch
with an iceberg?**
Cold spells.

**What do you get if
you cross a dinosaur
with a wizard?**
Tyrannosaurus hex.

What type of car does a ghost drive?
A Boo-ick.

What do young ghosts call their moms and dads?
Transparents.

What do you call two witches who live together?
Broommates.

What is a vampire's favorite sport?

Casketball.

How do ghosts make a milk shake?

They sneak up behind a glass of milk and yell, "Boo!"

What did the mother ghost say to her son?
"Don't spook unless you are spoken to."

Why was the witch kicked out of witching school?
Because she failed spell-ing.

Why are pixies such messy eaters?
Because they are always goblin their food.

How do you keep a monster from biting his nails?
Give him some screws.

**Why did Dracula
go to the doctor?**
Because of his coffin.

**What is a ghost's
favorite form of
transportation?**
A scare-plane.

**Why do vampires
need mouthwash?**
They have bat breath.

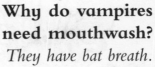

Why did the vampire subscribe to the *Wall Street Journal*?
He heard it had great circulation.

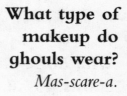

What type of makeup do ghouls wear?
Mas-scare-a.

What story do little witches like to hear at bedtime?
Ghoul deluxe and the three scares!

Why did the headless horseman go into business?
He wanted to get a head in life.

Why do female ghosts go on diets?
So that they can keep their ghoulish figures.

What should you say when you meet a ghost?
"How do you boo?"

What is a ghoul's favorite drink?
Lemon and slime.

Where do fashionable ghosts shop for sheets?
At boo-tiques.

Where does Dracula stay when he's in New York City?
The Vampire State Building.

Why were ancient Egyptian children confused?
Because their daddies were mummies!

How can you tell that a vampire likes baseball?
Every night he turns into a bat.

Who was the most famous French skeleton?
Napoleon Bone-apart.

What type of music do ghosts prefer?
Spirituals.

What is a vampire's favorite form of transportation?
A blood vessel.

What do you get if you cross a ghost with an owl?

Something that scares people and doesn't give a hoot.

What do you call a wizard from outer space?

A flying sorcerer.

What does a ghoul get when it comes home late for dinner?
The cold shoulder.

Why isn't Dracula invited to many parties?
He's a pain in the neck.

Why are ghosts like newspapers?
Because they appear in sheets.

How do monsters tell their future?
They read their horror-scopes.

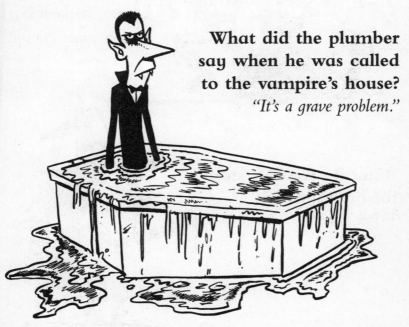

What did the plumber say when he was called to the vampire's house?
"It's a grave problem."

What is a ghost's favorite party game?
Musical graves.

Who did the ghost invite to his party?
Anyone that he could dig up.

What do wizards stop for on highways?
Witchhikers.

**What keeps
ghouls happy?**
*The knowledge that
every shroud has a
silver lining!*

**Who does
Dracula get
letters from?**
His fang club.

Count Dracula
Castle Drac
Transylvania

**What happened
when the ghosts
went on strike?**
*A skeleton crew
took over.*

STRIKE

What does Dracula drink with breakfast?

Coffin with scream and sugar.

What did the ghost teacher say to her class?

"Watch the board, and I'll go through it again!"

What would you get if you crossed a vampire with a snail?

I don't know, but it would slow him down.

Why did the twin witches wear name tags?

To tell which witch was which!

What is a ghost's favorite holiday?

April Ghouls' Day.

Which airline do ghouls fly with?
British Scare-ways!

What happened when the ghost met the zombie?
It was love at first fright.

What do little ghosts wear when it rains?
Boo-ts and ghoul-oshes!

What do you call a prehistoric ghost?
A terror-dactyl!

What is Dracula's favorite type of coffee?
De-coffin-ated.

What type of jewels do ghouls wear?
Gravestones!

What happened to the guy who didn't pay his exorcist?
He was repossessed.

Why can't skeletons play music in church?
Because they have no organs.

**What do you give a
vampire with a cold?**
Coffin drops.

**Where do ghosts
go on vacation?**
Mali-boo.

**What goes
"Ha, ha, ha—thud?"**
*A monster laughing
his head off.*

What do you call a dead cow that has come back to life?
Zombeef.

Where do ghosts go swimming?
The Dead Sea.

What does a vampire never order at a restaurant?
A stake sandwich.

What do demons have for breakfast?
Deviled eggs.

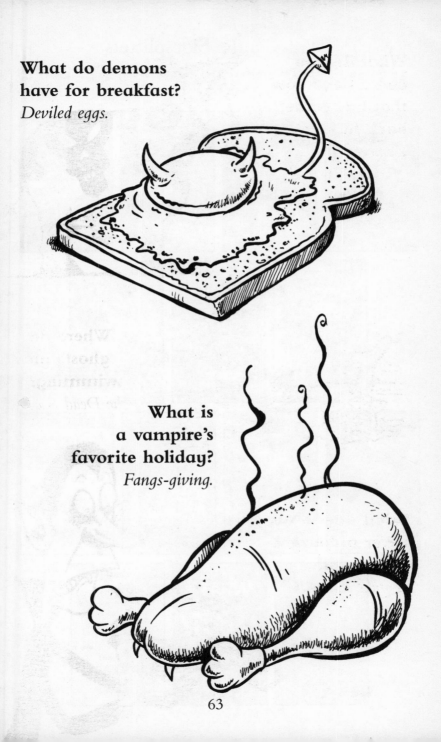

What is a vampire's favorite holiday?
Fangs-giving.

Titles in the **Sidesplitters** series you might enjoy: